P9-CAN-849

·TELL ME ABOUT·

BUILDINGS BRIDGES & TUNNELS

SERIES EDITOR: JACKIE GAFF

Warwick Press

Published in 1991 by Warwick Press,
387 Park Avenue South, New York, N.Y. 10016.
First published in 1991 by Kingfisher Books.

6 5 4 3 2 1

Printed in Spain

Library of Congress Cataloging-in-Publication Data
Royston, Angela.
Buildings, bridges, and tunnels / Angela Royston.
p. cm.—(Tell me about)
Includes index.
Summary: Uses question and answer format with pictures to explain elements and principles of structural engineering, the field that includes the design and construction of bridges, tunnels, and buildings. Shows how readers can build their own structures to scale.
ISBN 0-531-19108-7
1. Structural engineering—Juvenile literature. 2. Bridges—Design and construction—Juvenile literature. 3. Tunnels—Design and construction—Juvenile literature. 4. Buildings—Design and construction—Juvenile literature. [1. Structural engineering. 2. Bridges—Design and construction. 3. Tunnels—Design and construction. 4. Buildings—Design and construction.] I. Title. II. Series: Tell me about (Warwick Press)
TA634.R68 1991
624—dc20
90-13023
CIP
AC

Contents

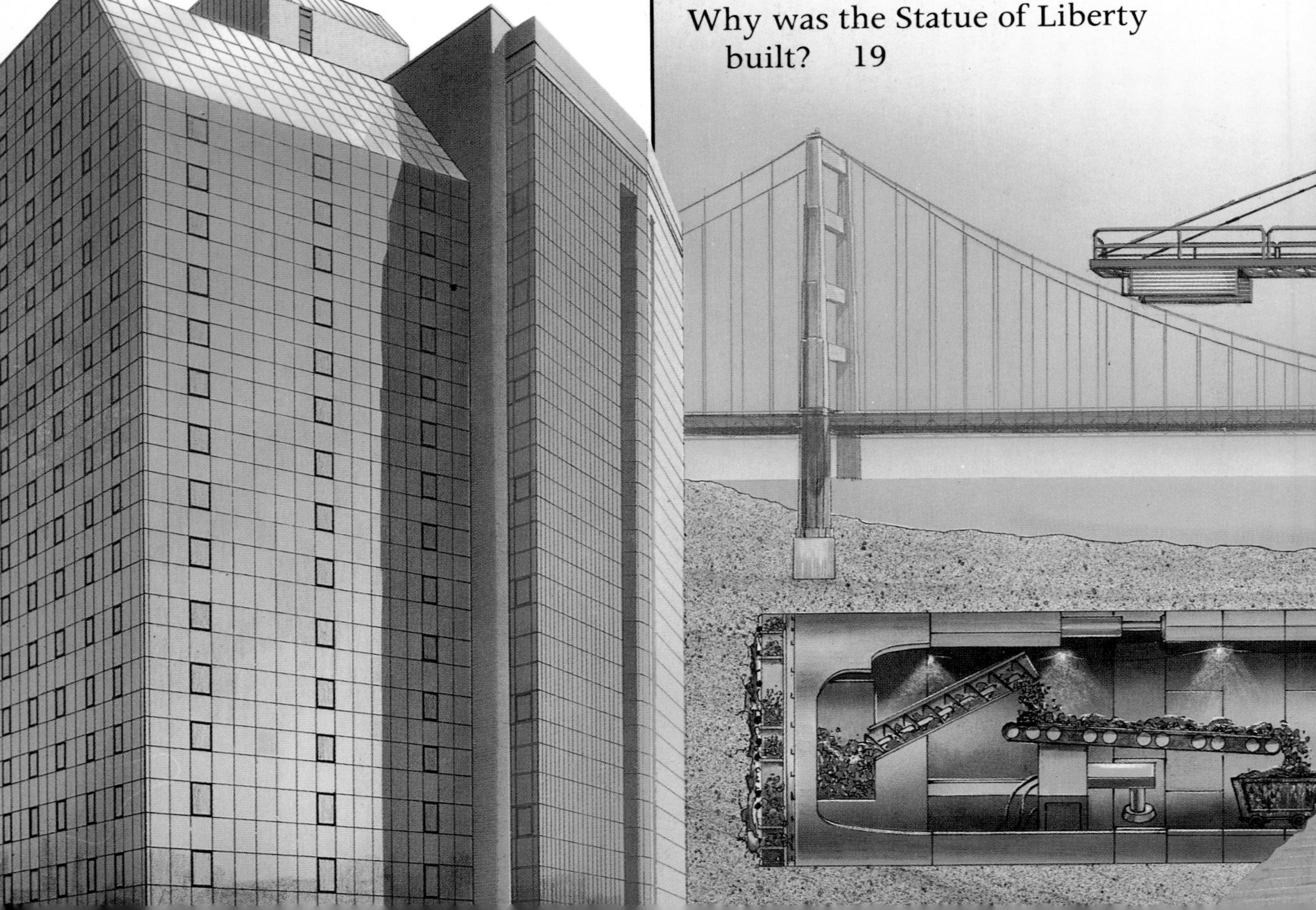

Why are buildings important?

Thousands of years ago, when people first started to build things, they used tree branches and animal skins to make huts to shelter them from harsh weather. Nowadays we build homes in all sorts of shapes and sizes, from towering apartment houses to single-story cottages. But big or small, these buildings are still important for the shelter and protection they give us.

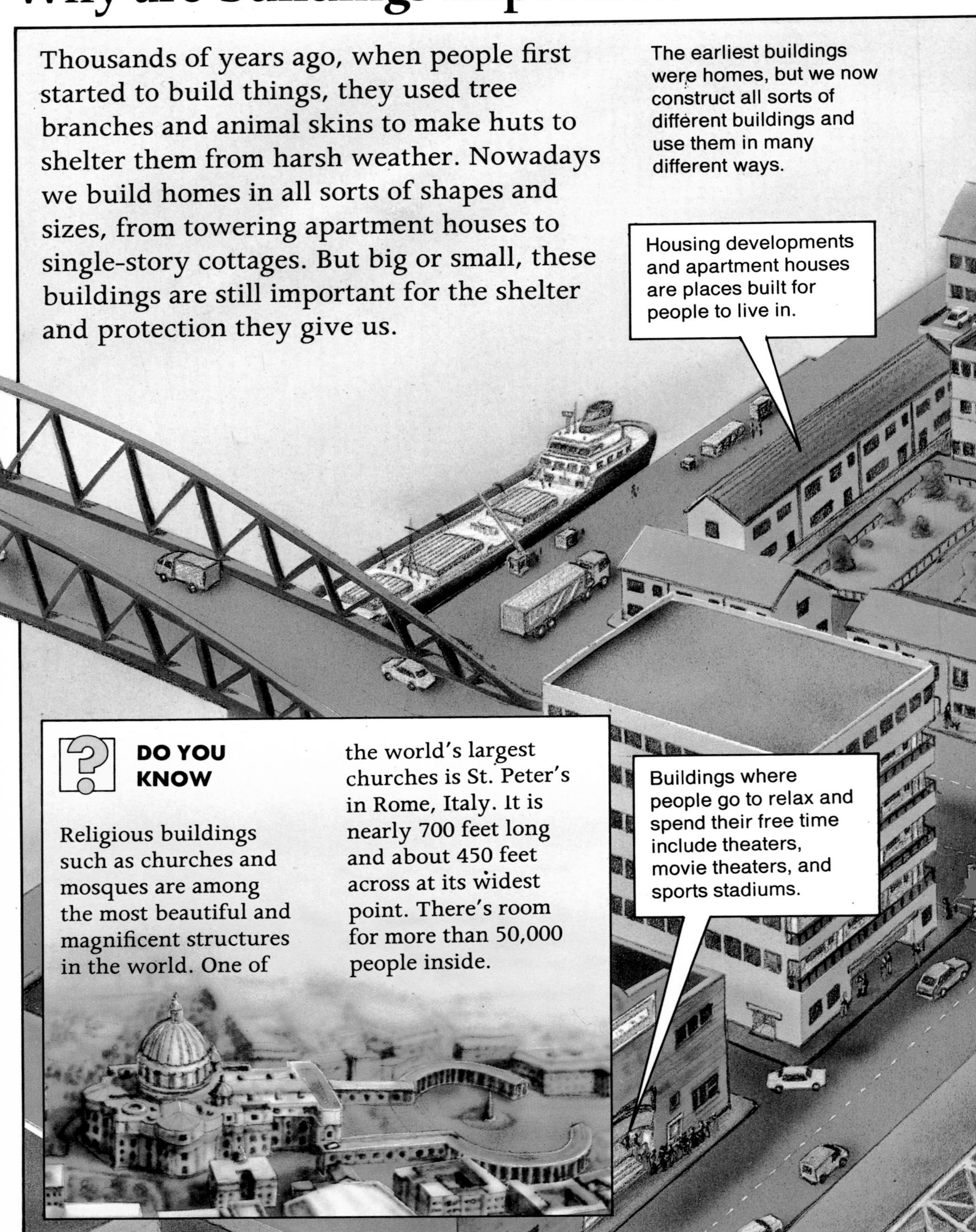

DO YOU KNOW

Religious buildings such as churches and mosques are among the most beautiful and magnificent structures in the world. One of the world's largest churches is St. Peter's in Rome, Italy. It is nearly 700 feet long and about 450 feet across at its widest point. There's room for more than 50,000 people inside.

DO YOU KNOW

The remains of the oldest homes in the world were discovered on a hillside in Nice, France, in the 1960s. The huts were built over 400,000 years ago, from wooden stakes supported by posts and heavy stones.

How are houses built?

Houses have to be designed and planned before building work begins, and architects are the people whose job it is to do this. The builders use the architect's plans as a guide while they are working on the house.

All modern buildings have foundations. These provide a firm base for the frame of the building, and they stop heavy structures from sinking into soft ground.

DESIGN A HOUSE

This is what an architect's plans are like. They show what the house will look like, inside and out. Use the plans as a model for designing a house of your own. How many rooms would you need? What would you use them for? Don't forget to put in windows, doors, and stairs!

BUILDING FACTS

- Concrete is a very hard building material which is sometimes used instead of bricks or stone, as well as for foundations. It's made by mixing sand, small stones, cement, and water. It sets like rock when dry.

- Bricks are made by baking clay at very high temperatures.

- Cement is made by mixing and burning clay and chalk, then grinding them into a fine powder. It's used in concrete and mortar.

- Mortar is used in wall-building to stick bricks and stones together. It's a gritty paste which dries hard. It's made by mixing sand, cement, and water.

Which are the largest houses?

The largest houses in the world are palaces where rulers such as kings and queens live. One of the world's largest private houses is Biltmore House in North Carolina. It has more than 250 rooms, including 32 guest bedrooms and its own gymnasium, swimming pool, and bowling alley!

Biltmore House was built for George W. Vanderbilt in 1890–95, in the style of 16th-century French châteaux, or castles. The Vanderbilt family no longer lives there, and the house and its beautiful gardens are open for the public to visit.

HOUSE FACTS

- A fisherman's cottage in Conwy, North Wales, is one of the world's smallest houses. It's less than 6 feet wide and just over 10 feet high. Inside it only has a staircase and two tiny rooms. Most adults wouldn't be able to stand up straight in them!

FISHERMAN'S COTTAGE, CONWY

- There are many large palaces throughout the world, but few are still lived in as homes. The largest palace which is still a home is that of the Sultan of Brunei, a tiny country in Southeast Asia. It has more than 1,780 rooms and 250 toilets!

Which are the tallest buildings?

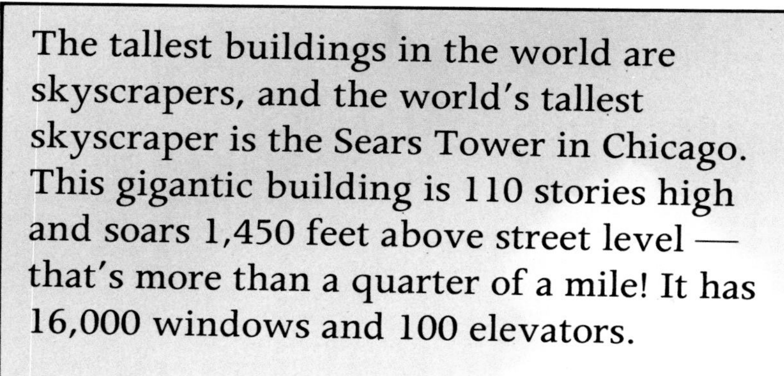

The tallest buildings in the world are skyscrapers, and the world's tallest skyscraper is the Sears Tower in Chicago. This gigantic building is 110 stories high and soars 1,450 feet above street level — that's more than a quarter of a mile! It has 16,000 windows and 100 elevators.

DO YOU KNOW

New York City has more skyscrapers than anywhere else in the world. Most of them are on the island of Manhattan.

1 Chrysler Building (1,050 feet high), New York, 1930.

2 Empire State Building (1,250 feet high), New York, 1931.

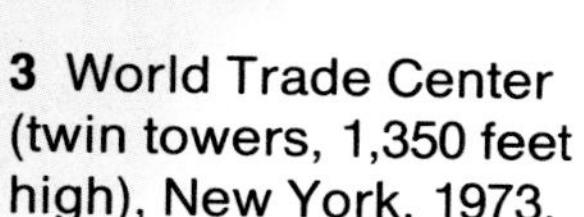

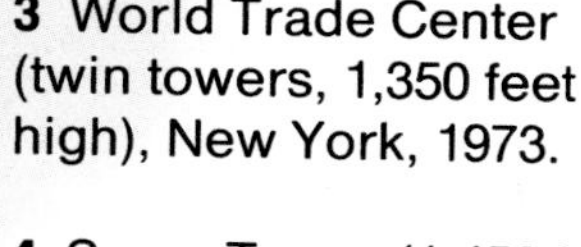

3 World Trade Center (twin towers, 1,350 feet high), New York, 1973.

4 Sears Tower (1,450 feet high), Chicago, 1974.

WIND TESTING

Did you know that tall buildings are designed to sway in high winds so that they don't shake themselves to pieces and fall down?

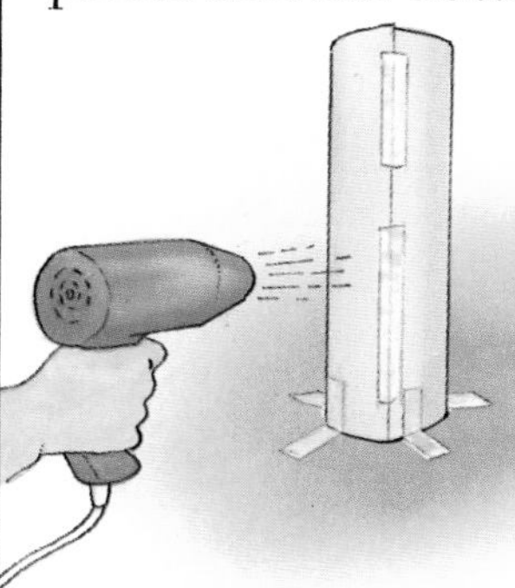

To see how wind affects tall buildings, make a long tube out of thin cardboard and tape its base to a table. Then use a hair dryer to blow "wind" at your tower.

How are skyscrapers built?

Skyscrapers are very heavy because they are so tall. This means that they need firm foundations to support their weight and a strong framework to hold them together. The framework of most skyscrapers is made from long metal beams called girders. The floors and walls are supported by the framework and can be added as each story is completed.

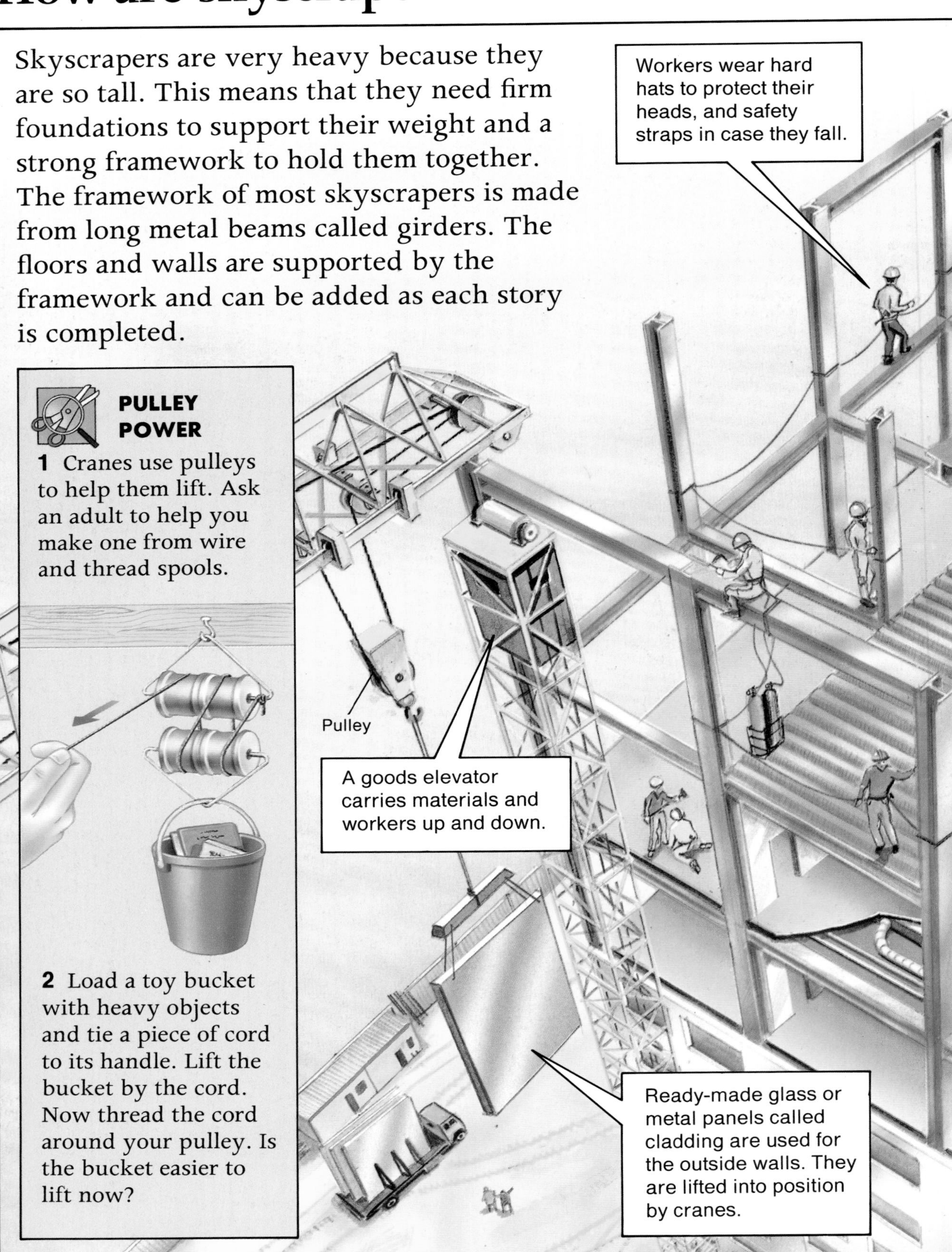

PULLEY POWER

1 Cranes use pulleys to help them lift. Ask an adult to help you make one from wire and thread spools.

2 Load a toy bucket with heavy objects and tie a piece of cord to its handle. Lift the bucket by the cord. Now thread the cord around your pulley. Is the bucket easier to lift now?

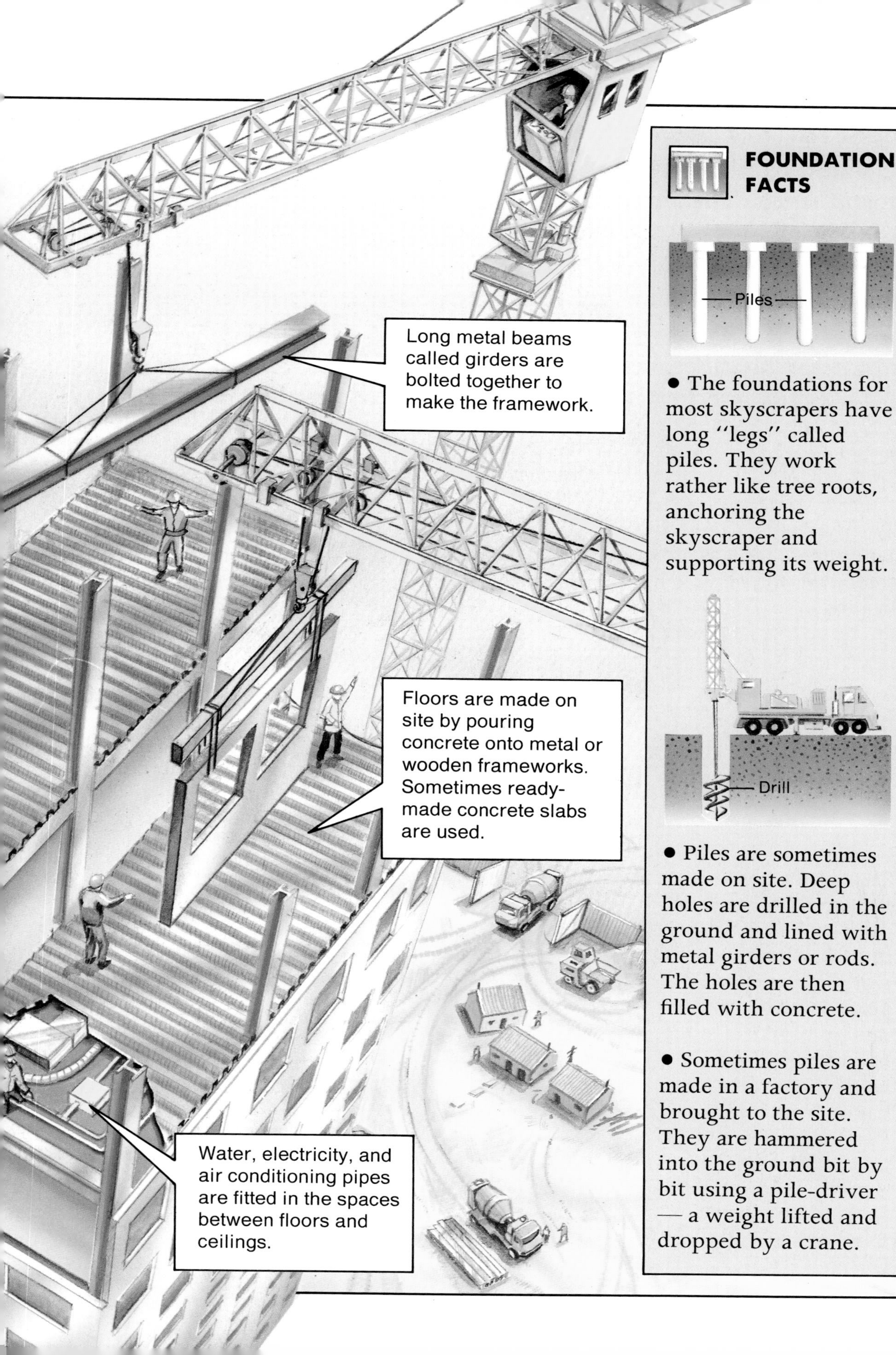

FOUNDATION FACTS

Piles

• The foundations for most skyscrapers have long "legs" called piles. They work rather like tree roots, anchoring the skyscraper and supporting its weight.

Drill

• Piles are sometimes made on site. Deep holes are drilled in the ground and lined with metal girders or rods. The holes are then filled with concrete.

• Sometimes piles are made in a factory and brought to the site. They are hammered into the ground bit by bit using a pile-driver — a weight lifted and dropped by a crane.

What were the Seven Wonders?

The Seven Wonders of the World were some of the most spectacular structures of ancient times. They were described over 2,000 years ago, by a Greek writer called Antipater of Sidon. Over the centuries, some of the Seven Wonders collapsed and fell into ruin. Others were destroyed by fires or earthquakes. Only the pyramids at Giza are still standing today.

1 The Giza pyramids were built about 4,500 years ago. They are the oldest of the Seven Wonders (the others were built 2,500–2,000 years ago), the only ones still standing.

DO YOU KNOW

The pyramids of Egypt were built as tombs for pharaohs, or kings.

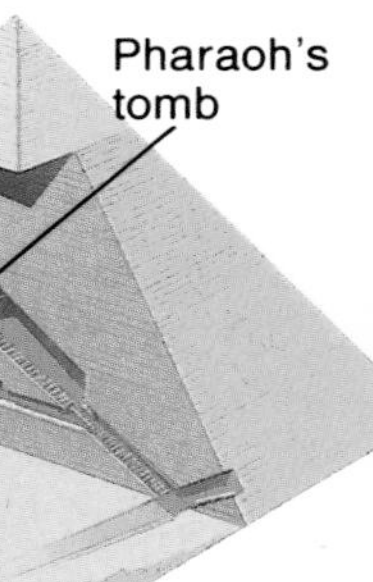

The largest, the Great Pyramid at Giza, was over 480 feet high and took thousands of workers more than 30 years to build. Over 2 million blocks of stone had to be cut and hauled into place by hand. People think that today it would take at least 400 workers using modern equipment more than five years to build it.

2 The greenery and flowers of the Hanging Gardens of Babylon were particularly amazing because they were created in the middle of the desert.

3 The Temple of Artemis at Ephesus was one of the largest temples of ancient times. Its columns were over six times the height of a man.

4 The Colossus of Rhodes was a huge bronze statue of the Greek sun god Helios. It was destroyed by an earthquake less than 60 years after it was completed.

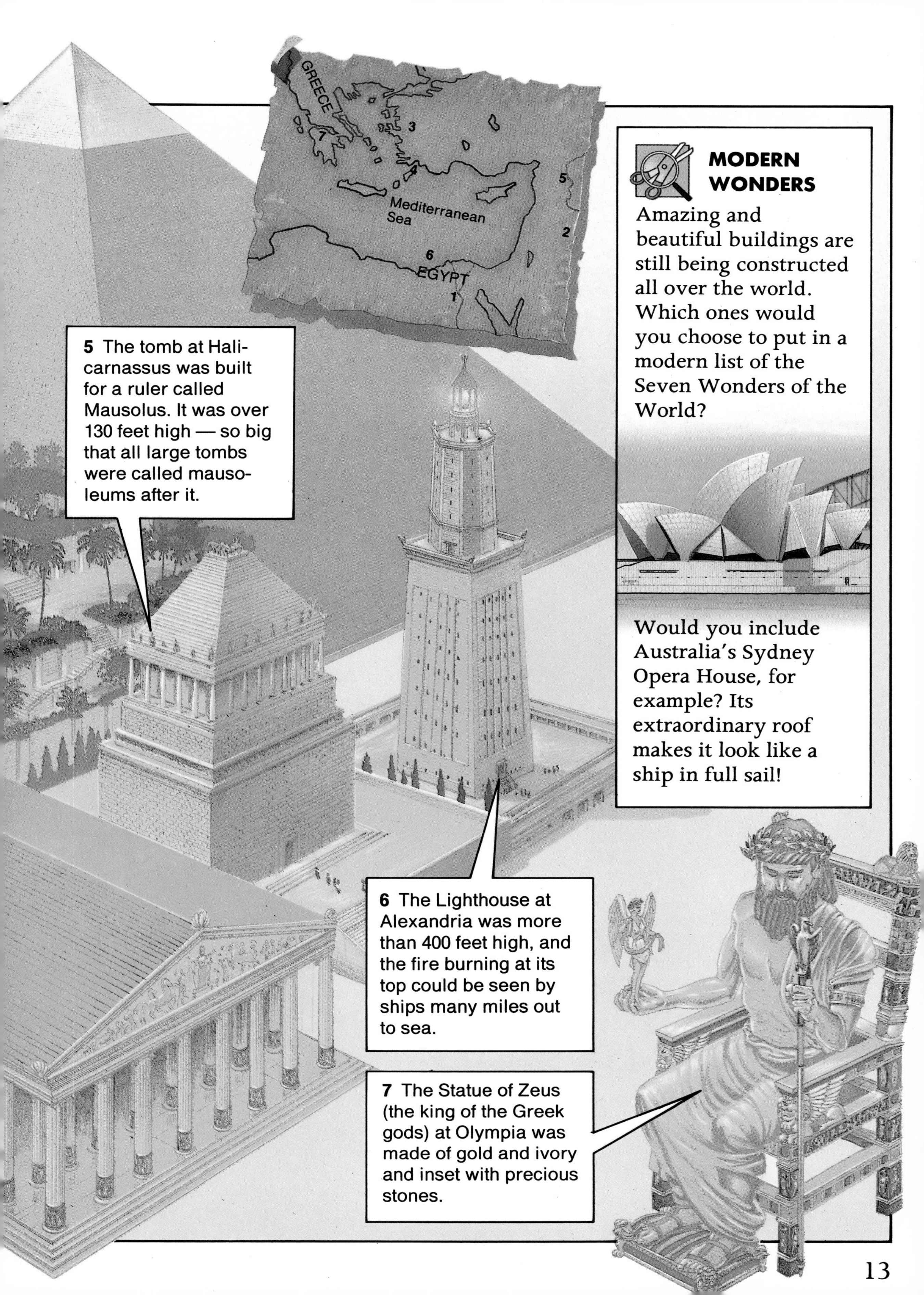

5 The tomb at Halicarnassus was built for a ruler called Mausolus. It was over 130 feet high — so big that all large tombs were called mausoleums after it.

6 The Lighthouse at Alexandria was more than 400 feet high, and the fire burning at its top could be seen by ships many miles out to sea.

7 The Statue of Zeus (the king of the Greek gods) at Olympia was made of gold and ivory and inset with precious stones.

MODERN WONDERS

Amazing and beautiful buildings are still being constructed all over the world. Which ones would you choose to put in a modern list of the Seven Wonders of the World?

Would you include Australia's Sydney Opera House, for example? Its extraordinary roof makes it look like a ship in full sail!

How long is the Great Wall of China?

At nearly 2,175 miles long — nearly as far as from Los Angeles to Washington D.C. — the Great Wall of China is the largest structure ever built. It was begun over 2,200 years ago, during the rule of the emperor Shi Huangdi, as a defense against fierce tribes which were trying to invade China from the north.

DO YOU KNOW

The Great Wall of China is the only structure built by people which can be seen from the Moon.

The Great Wall winds across the mountains and valleys of northern China for nearly 2,200 miles. It has more than 1,770 miles of additional, branching walls.

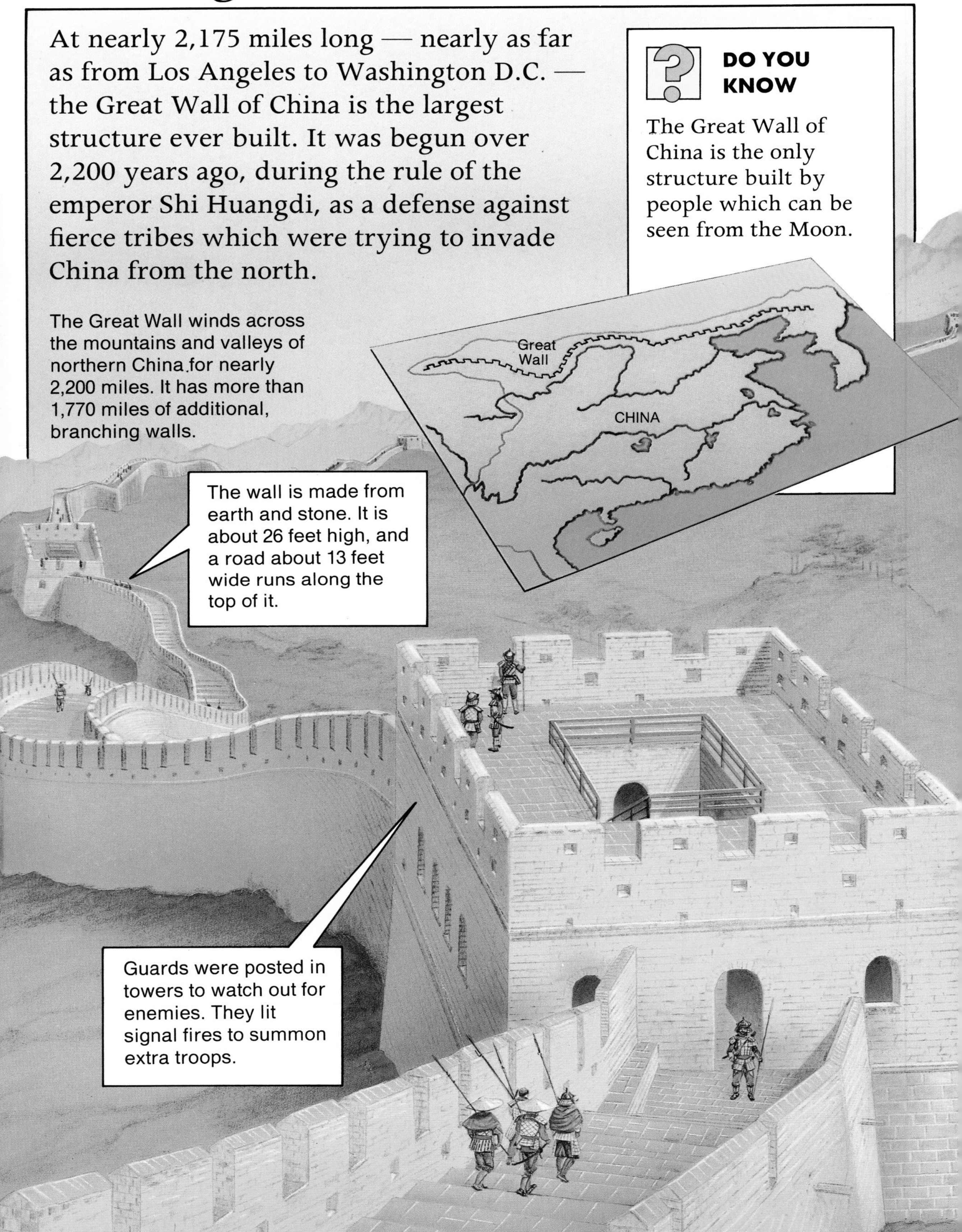

The wall is made from earth and stone. It is about 26 feet high, and a road about 13 feet wide runs along the top of it.

Guards were posted in towers to watch out for enemies. They lit signal fires to summon extra troops.

Who built the Parthenon?

The Parthenon was built by the Ancient Greeks over 2,300 years ago, as a temple for the goddess Athena. Its ruins are still standing today, on a hill called the Acropolis in the Greek city of Athens.

The Ancient Greeks used rows of thick stone pillars called columns to support beams and roofs.

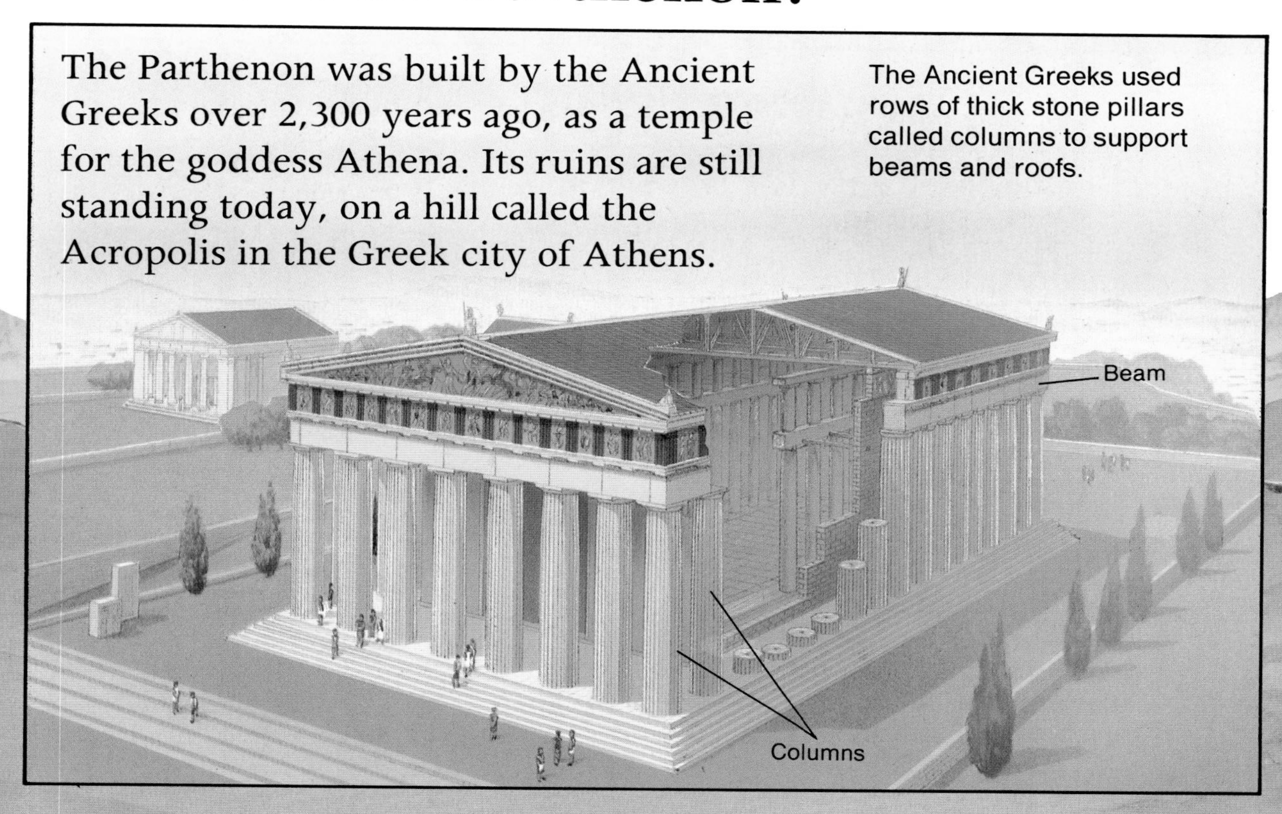

Who built the Colosseum?

The Colosseum is in Rome, the capital city of Italy. It was built by the Romans nearly 2,000 years ago, as a giant sports arena — it had seating for nearly 50,000 people!

Romans went to the Colosseum to see men called gladiators fighting each other. Gladiators also fought wild animals such as lions.

DO YOU KNOW

The Romans were able to construct bigger and stronger buildings than the Ancient Greeks because they learned how to use arches. These can carry more weight than columns and beams.

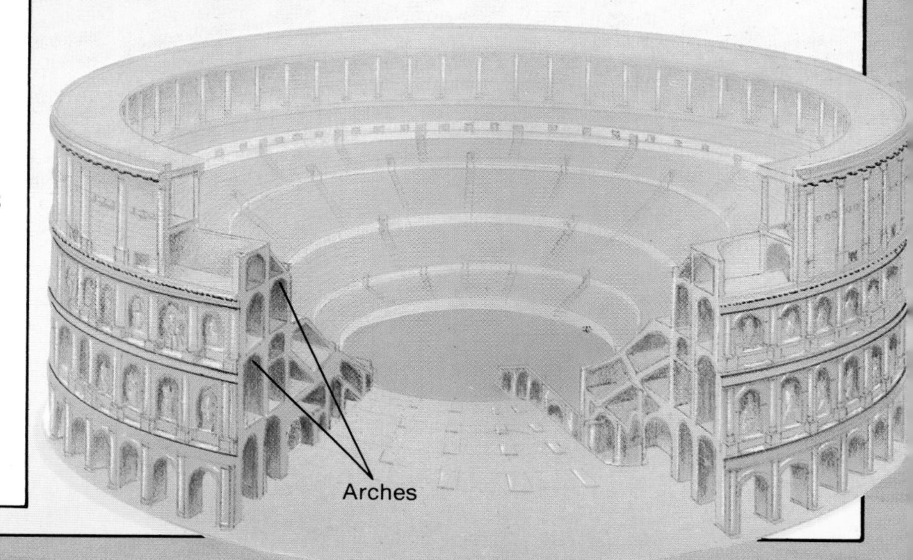

How were castles built?

European kings and lords began building stone castles about 1,000 years ago, to protect themselves and their lands from enemies. Because castles were designed to resist enemy attack, they had very high thick walls — up to 12 times the height of a man and 12 to 20 feet thick.

Workers had simple tools in those days, so castle-building took a long time. Around 1,000 people would have worked for ten years building a medium-sized castle.

CASTLE FACTS

- The largest castle in the world that people still live in is Windsor Castle, which belongs to the British royal family. It covers roughly the same area as 12 football fields!
- The Kremlin in Moscow in the U.S.S.R., was built over 500 years ago for the Russian tsars, or kings. It has 20 towers and its pink walls rise to over 60 feet.
- Castles weren't just built in Europe. Japanese lords began building stone castles about 450 years ago, for example. The walls of their castles often sloped inward.

Why does the Tower of Pisa lean?

This famous Italian building started tilting to one side as soon as its first three stories were completed. Its foundations aren't strong enough to support its weight, and it started leaning as it began sinking into the soft ground beneath it.

The tower is still tilting, at a rate of about five hundredths of an inch a year. Its top is now nearly 16 feet to one side of its base.

DO YOU KNOW

The Tower of Pisa was built in 1173–1372, as a church bell tower. No one rings the bells now, though, as the clanging might make the tower lean faster.

Why was the Eiffel Tower built?

In 1889, a huge international exhibition of art and trade objects was held in Paris, the capital city of France. The Eiffel Tower was built for this exhibition. At that time it was the tallest structure in the world.

The Eiffel Tower is 984 feet high — taller than 40 two-story houses! Its strong metal framework is made of iron.

DO YOU KNOW

At just over 2,100 feet high, the Warszawa radio mast in Poland is the world's tallest structure. It's held up and strengthened by metal cables.

Why was the Statue of Liberty built?

The Statue of Liberty was given to the U.S.A. by the people of France in 1884, to celebrate the friendship between the two countries and their belief in the importance of liberty, or freedom. The statue was built in France, then taken apart and shipped across to the U.S.A., where it was rebuilt on an island in New York Harbor.

DO YOU KNOW

The world's tallest statue is just over 270 feet high — nearly twice as high as the Statue of Liberty. It's called Motherland, and it's on a hill outside the city of Volgograd in south-eastern U.S.S.R.

Why do people build bridges?

Bridges make journeys shorter, easier, and safer. They allow us to cross natural barriers such as wide rivers and deep ravines and gorges, for example, and to travel safely over busy roads and railways. Bridges can also be used instead of traffic lights at road junctions, to speed the flow of cars and trucks, and to avoid traffic jams.

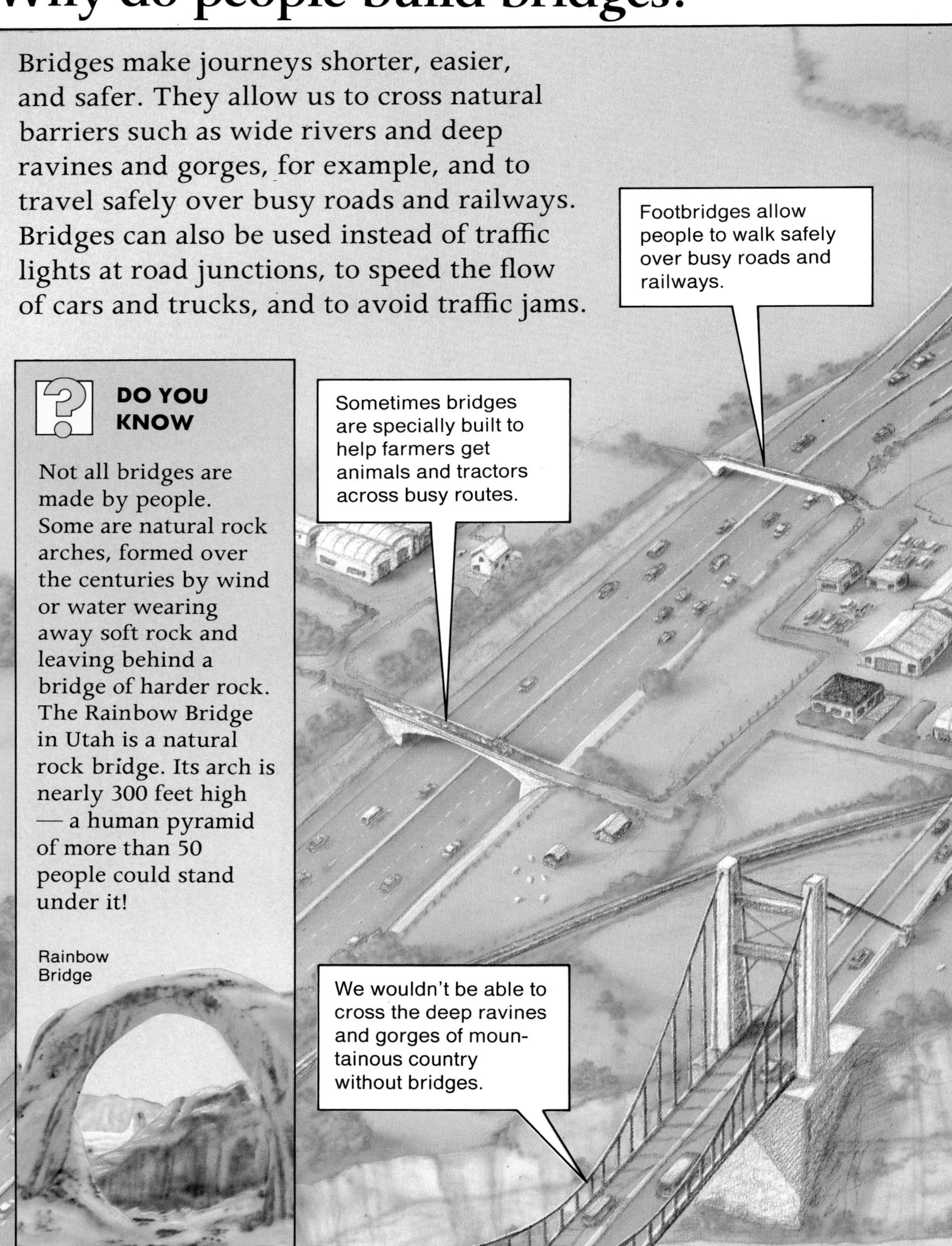

DO YOU KNOW

Not all bridges are made by people. Some are natural rock arches, formed over the centuries by wind or water wearing away soft rock and leaving behind a bridge of harder rock. The Rainbow Bridge in Utah is a natural rock bridge. Its arch is nearly 300 feet high — a human pyramid of more than 50 people could stand under it!

Rainbow Bridge

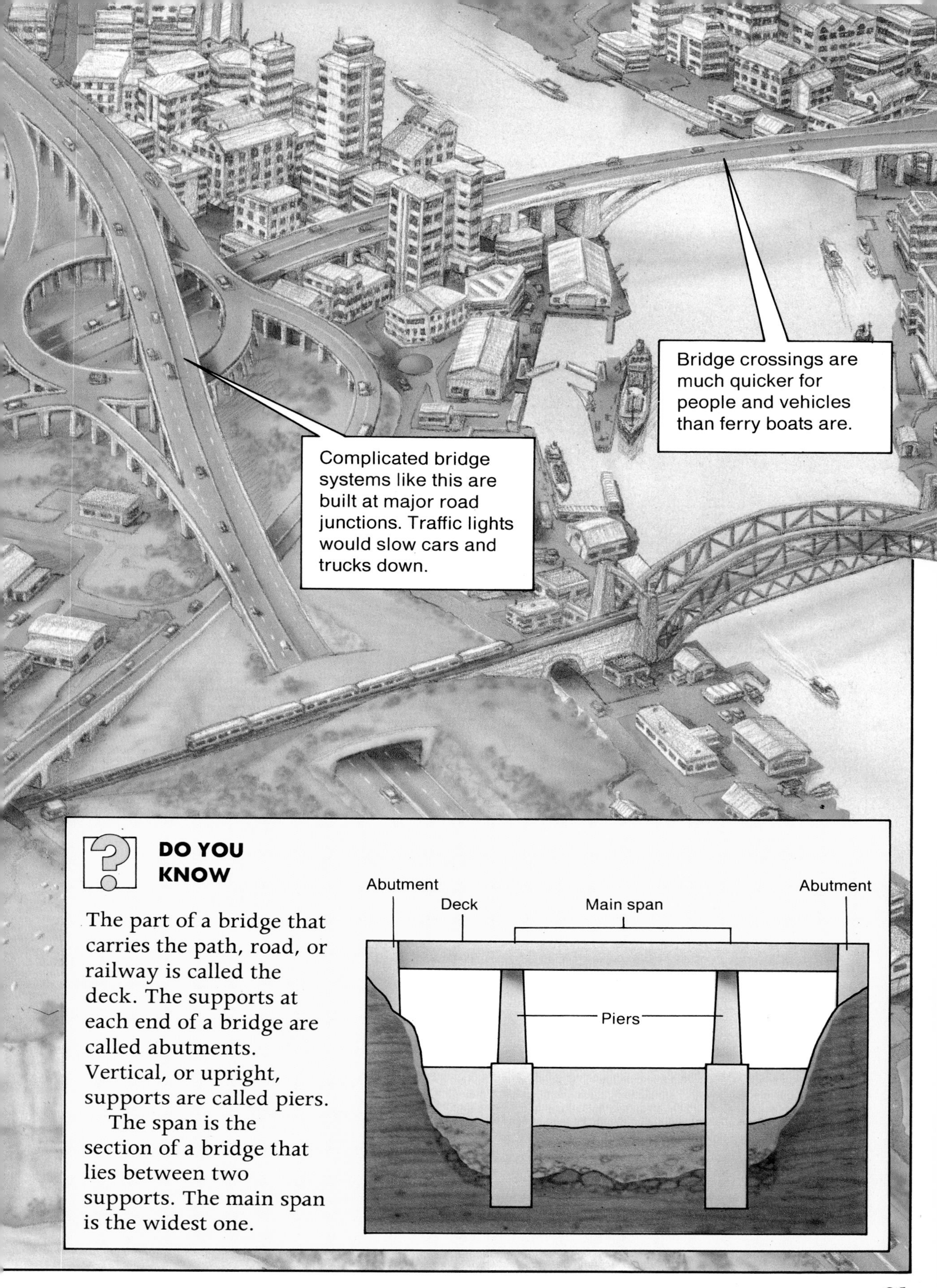

Bridge crossings are much quicker for people and vehicles than ferry boats are.

Complicated bridge systems like this are built at major road junctions. Traffic lights would slow cars and trucks down.

DO YOU KNOW

The part of a bridge that carries the path, road, or railway is called the deck. The supports at each end of a bridge are called abutments. Vertical, or upright, supports are called piers.

The span is the section of a bridge that lies between two supports. The main span is the widest one.

What types of bridge are there?

There are three basic types of bridge — beam, arch, and suspension. The fourth bridge illustrated below, the cantilever, is a type of beam bridge. Beam bridges are very common — you may have made one yourself, by laying a plank or a log across a stream.

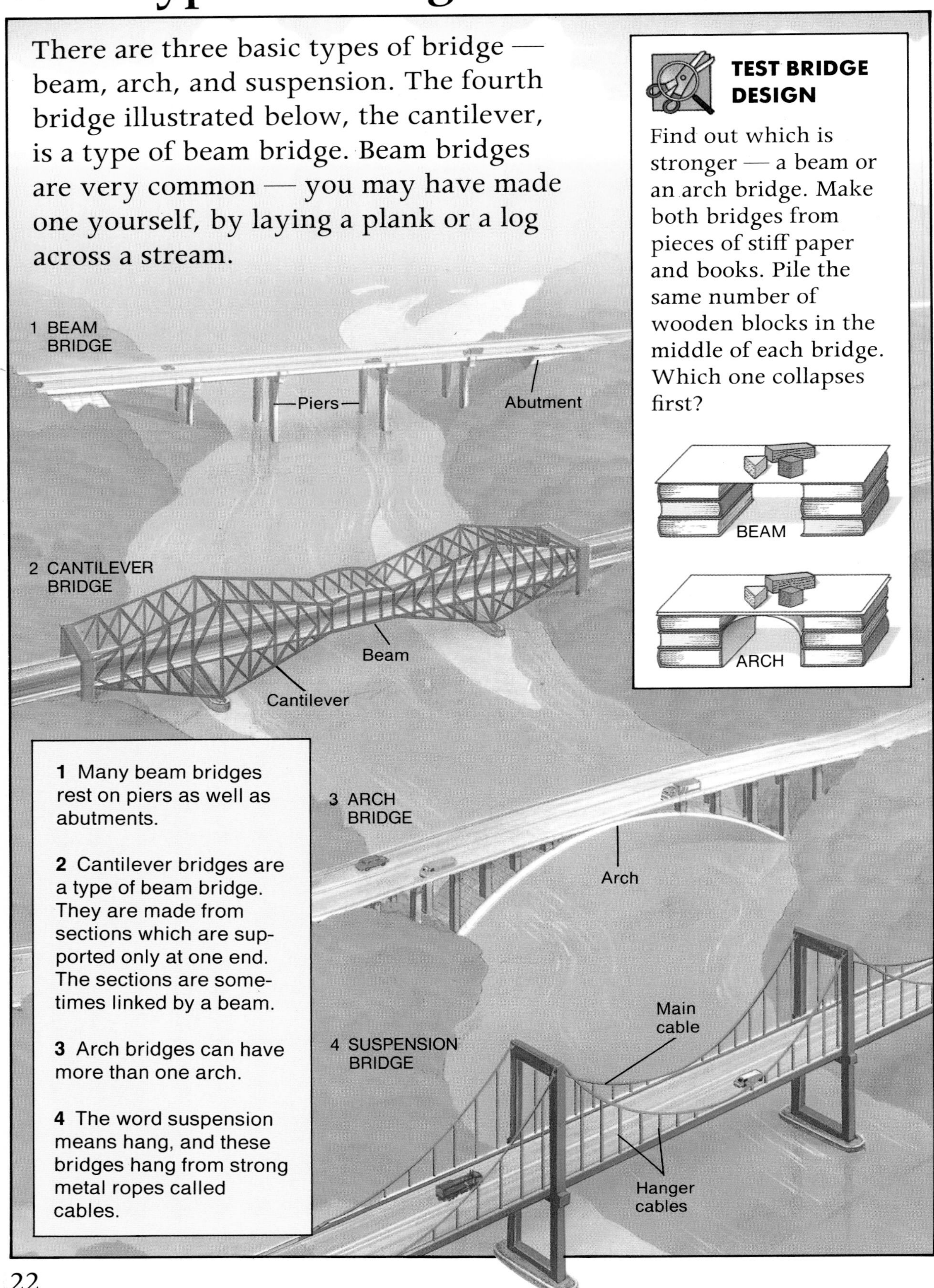

TEST BRIDGE DESIGN

Find out which is stronger — a beam or an arch bridge. Make both bridges from pieces of stiff paper and books. Pile the same number of wooden blocks in the middle of each bridge. Which one collapses first?

1 Many beam bridges rest on piers as well as abutments.

2 Cantilever bridges are a type of beam bridge. They are made from sections which are supported only at one end. The sections are sometimes linked by a beam.

3 Arch bridges can have more than one arch.

4 The word suspension means hang, and these bridges hang from strong metal ropes called cables.

Can bridges move?

Some river bridges are designed to allow large ships to pass through them. Tower Bridge over the River Thames in London is this type of bridge. Its deck, or roadway, is in two parts, which can be raised high above the river. Bridges like Tower Bridge are called bascules or drawbridges. They were first used over castle moats.

MOVING BRIDGE FACTS

- The deck of some bridges swings sideways, to allow ships to pass on either side.
- On other bridges, the whole deck can be raised straight up between two towers so ships can sail beneath.

How are suspension bridges built?

With their tall slender towers and long main spans, suspension bridges are among the world's most beautiful and impressive structures. Like all bridges, though, they have to be strong enough to carry their own weight, as well as that of the people and vehicles that use them. The weight of a suspension bridge is carried by its two main cables, so these have to be anchored very firmly into the ground.

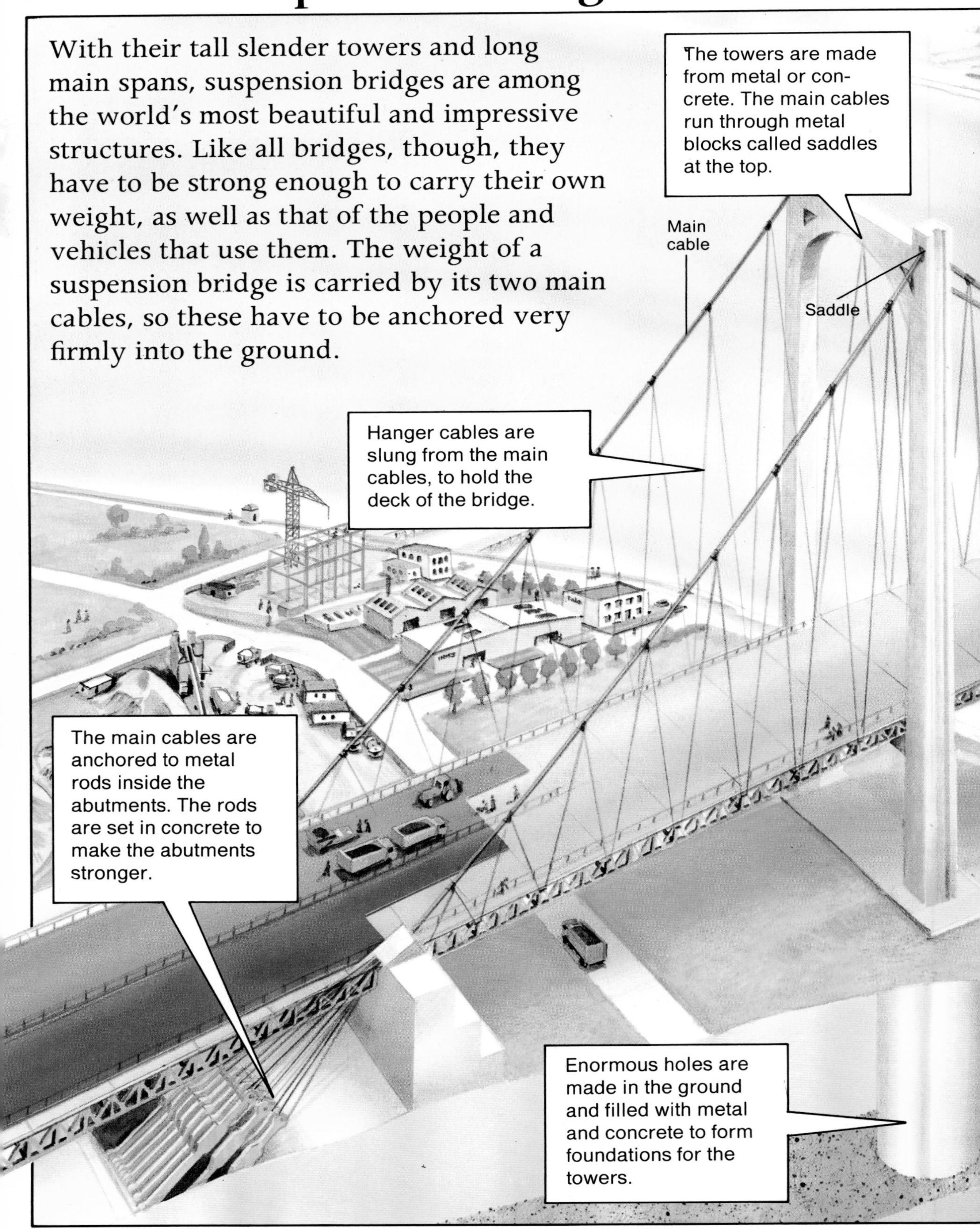

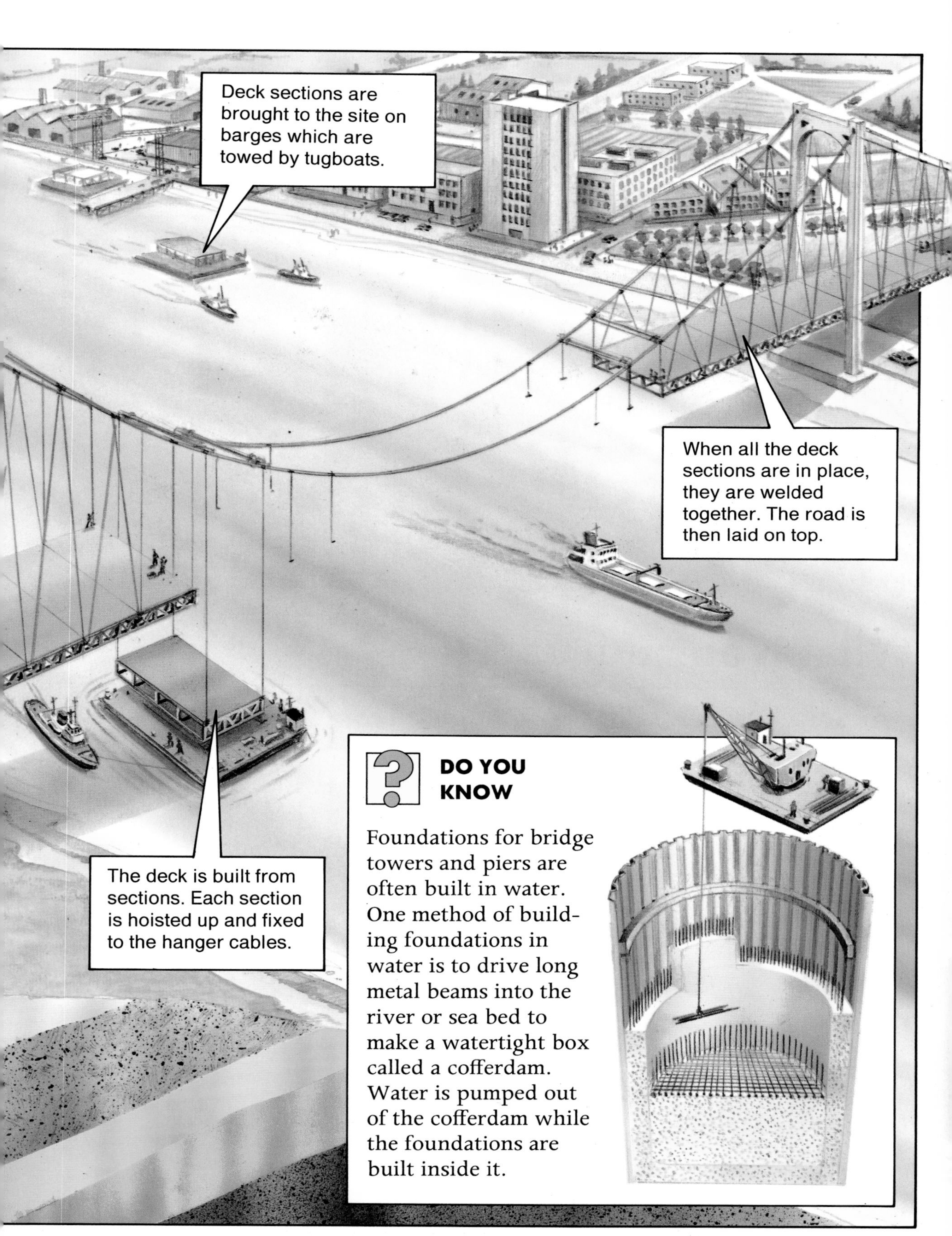
Deck sections are brought to the site on barges which are towed by tugboats.
When all the deck sections are in place, they are welded together. The road is then laid on top.
The deck is built from sections. Each section is hoisted up and fixed to the hanger cables.
DO YOU KNOW
Foundations for bridge towers and piers are often built in water. One method of building foundations in water is to drive long metal beams into the river or sea bed to make a watertight box called a cofferdam. Water is pumped out of the cofferdam while the foundations are built inside it.

Which are the oldest bridges?

The clapper bridges of southwest England are thought to be the oldest bridges in the world that are still standing, but it isn't possible to date them exactly. The oldest datable bridge was built nearly 3,000 years ago, across the River Meles in Turkey.

Clapper bridges were built thousands of years ago, from large stone slabs placed on top of boulders.

DO YOU KNOW

A Greek historian called Herodotus, who lived nearly 2,500 years ago, described a bridge of boats built for the invading armies of King Xerxes of Persia (in western Asia). Two bridges were built side by side, using 674 boats which were tied together by ropes and firmly anchored. Floating bridges are called pontoons.

What is an aqueduct?

An aqueduct is a bridge which is specially designed to carry water. The Romans were great bridge builders, and many of their aqueducts are still standing.

The Pont du Gard was built by the Romans nearly 2,000 years ago. It is part of an aqueduct system which carried water more than 25 miles to supply the city of Nîmes in southern France.

When did people live on bridges?

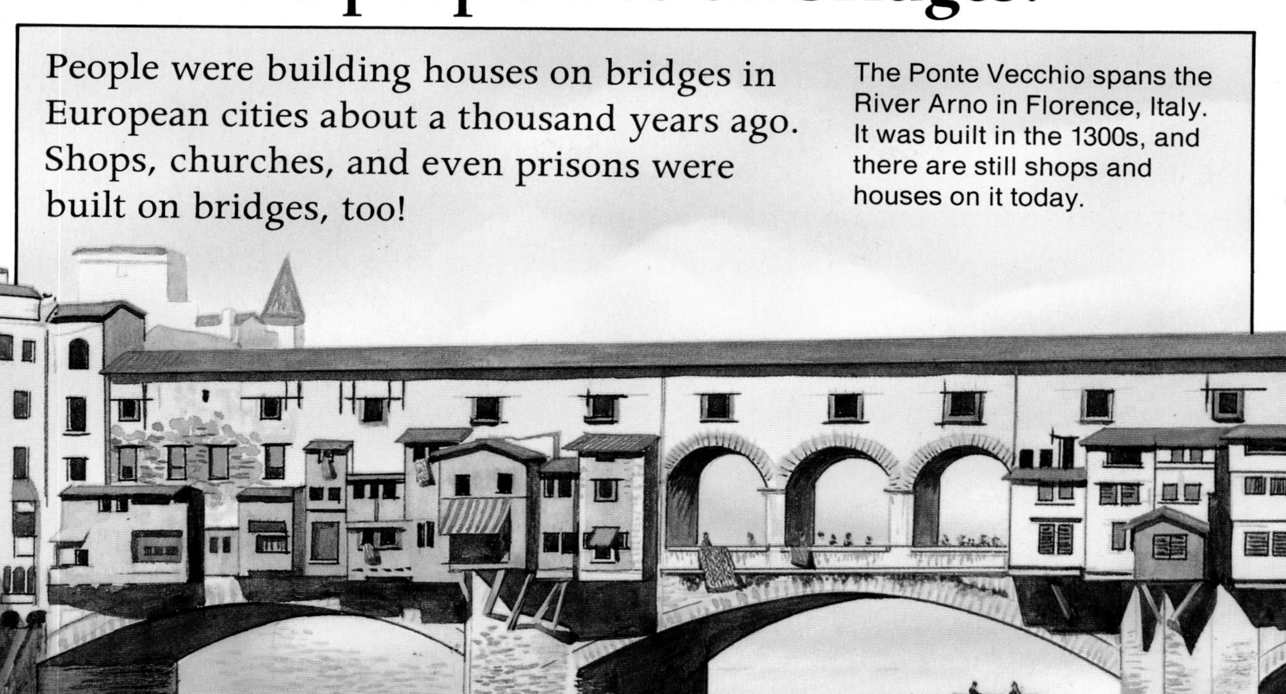

People were building houses on bridges in European cities about a thousand years ago. Shops, churches, and even prisons were built on bridges, too!

The Ponte Vecchio spans the River Arno in Florence, Italy. It was built in the 1300s, and there are still shops and houses on it today.

Where is the Bridge of Sighs?

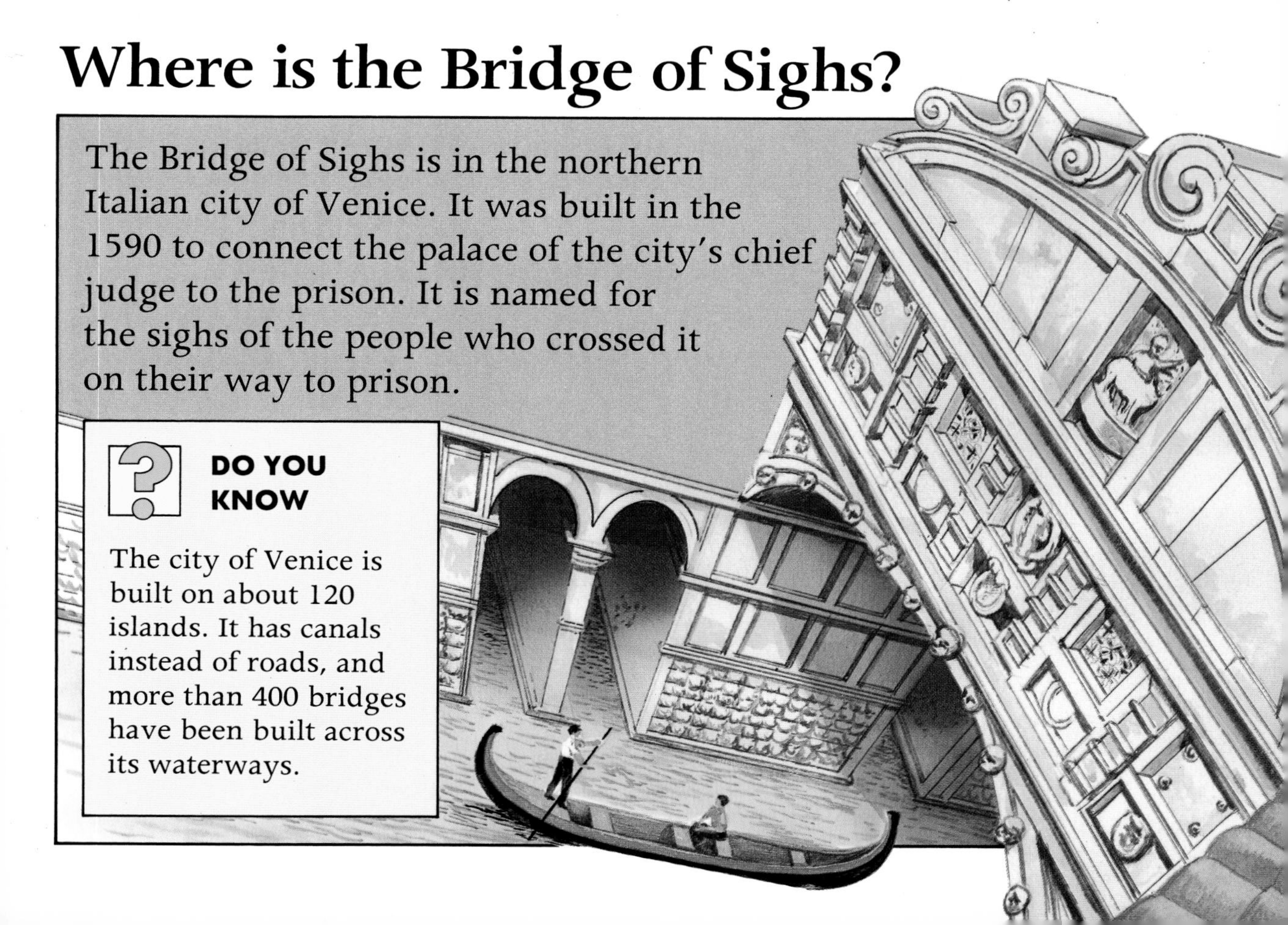

The Bridge of Sighs is in the northern Italian city of Venice. It was built in the 1590 to connect the palace of the city's chief judge to the prison. It is named for the sighs of the people who crossed it on their way to prison.

DO YOU KNOW

The city of Venice is built on about 120 islands. It has canals instead of roads, and more than 400 bridges have been built across its waterways.

Which is the longest bridge?

The world's longest bridging crosses Lake Pontchartrain in Louisiana. There are two causeways, and they're so long that you can't see land from the middle of them — together they measure nearly 48 miles!

The bridge with the longest span crosses the River Humber in northern England. It's a suspension bridge, and its main span is 4,626 feet long.

The world's first all-iron bridge was built over the River Severn in the English Midlands in 1779.

The Humber Estuary Bridge was opened in 1981. Drivers have to pay a toll when crossing it.

The towers are 533 feet high. They are made from concrete strengthened with metal rods.

The overall length of the bridge is 7,280 feet. Its main span measures 4,626 feet.

BRIDGE OF KNIVES

1 Amaze your friends with this building trick. Challenge them to use three long-bladed table knives and three glasses to build a bridge strong enough to support a fourth glass.

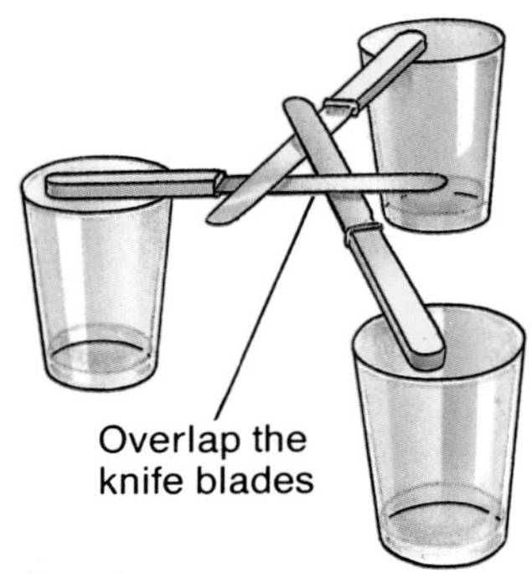

Overlap the knife blades

2 The secret to success lies in the way the knife blades lock together, as the illustration above shows!

Which is the widest bridge?

The Sydney Harbour Bridge is the widest long-span bridge in the world. Its main span measures 160 feet across and is 1,650 feet long. The bridge is a steel arch and it opened in 1932. Sydney is the capital of the Australian state of New South Wales.

The Sydney Harbour Bridge carries two railroad tracks and eight traffic lanes as well as a footpath. It is 160 feet wide.

Which is the highest bridge?

The highest bridge in the world crosses the Royal Gorge of the Arkansas River in Colorado. This graceful suspension bridge towers 1,053 feet above the surface of the river — the Eiffel Tower would fit comfortably beneath it!

The Arkansas River Bridge carries road traffic and is the world's highest bridge. It was built in 1929 — in just six months!

Why do people build tunnels?

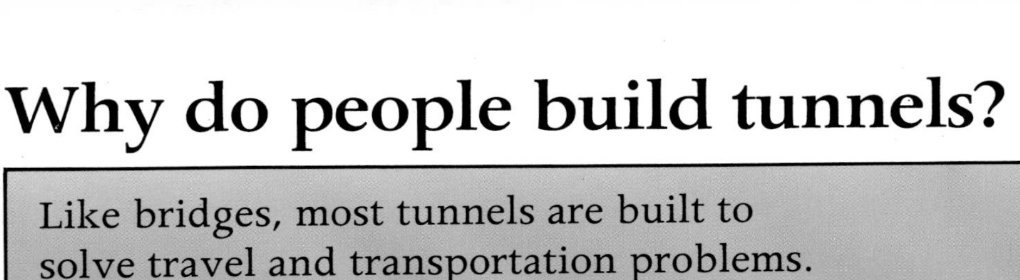

Like bridges, most tunnels are built to solve travel and transportation problems. By burrowing through steep mountains, below wide rivers, and beneath busy city streets, tunnels make it quicker and easier for us to get from one place to another — whether on foot, or in cars or trains.

TEST TUNNEL DESIGN

Most tunnels have arched roofs, because this shape is stronger than a square. Here's a way to compare the strength of arches and squares.

1 You'll need a cardboard tube and a box with a lid. Put them in damp sand. Mold more damp sand firmly around them.

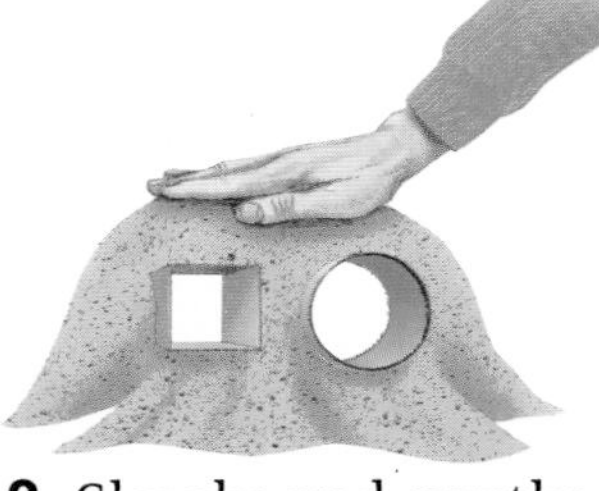

2 Slowly and gently, slide the box and the tube out of the sand. Now press down on the sand above each tunnel until it collapses. Which tunnel caved in first, the arch or the square?

DO YOU KNOW

The roof of a tunnel is called the crown. Its entrance or mouth is called the portal.

Tunnels are often built to carry people and traffic quickly beneath rivers.

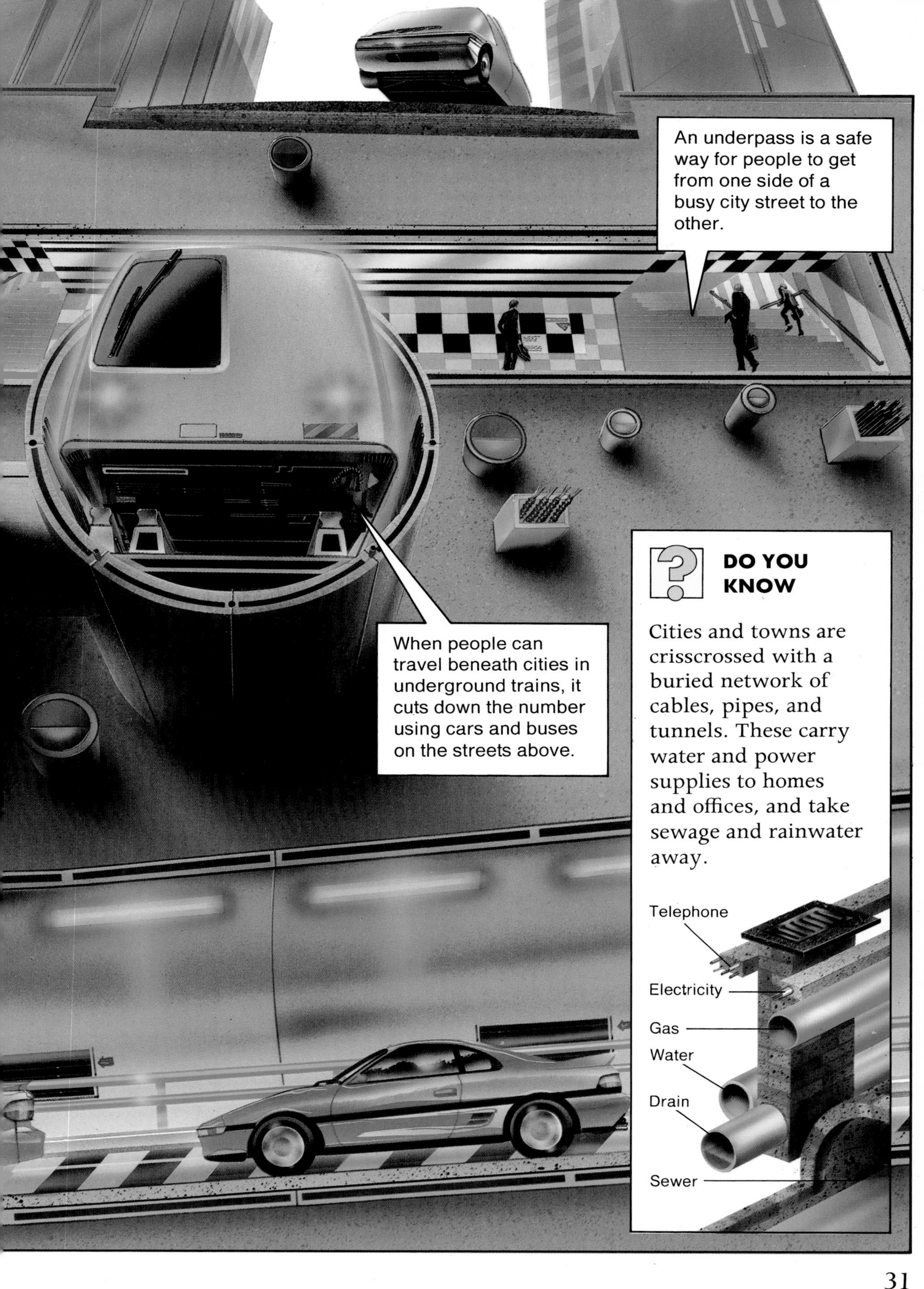

DO YOU KNOW

Cities and towns are crisscrossed with a buried network of cables, pipes, and tunnels. These carry water and power supplies to homes and offices, and take sewage and rainwater away.

How are tunnels bored?

Before work starts on boring a tunnel, scientists carry out tests to find out what the soil and rock are like along its route. If the scientists discover that the rock is soft and firm — chalk, for example — a tunnel-boring machine (TBM) similar to the one below is used. TBMs are like giant drills, which bore tunnels through rock as they rotate, or turn.

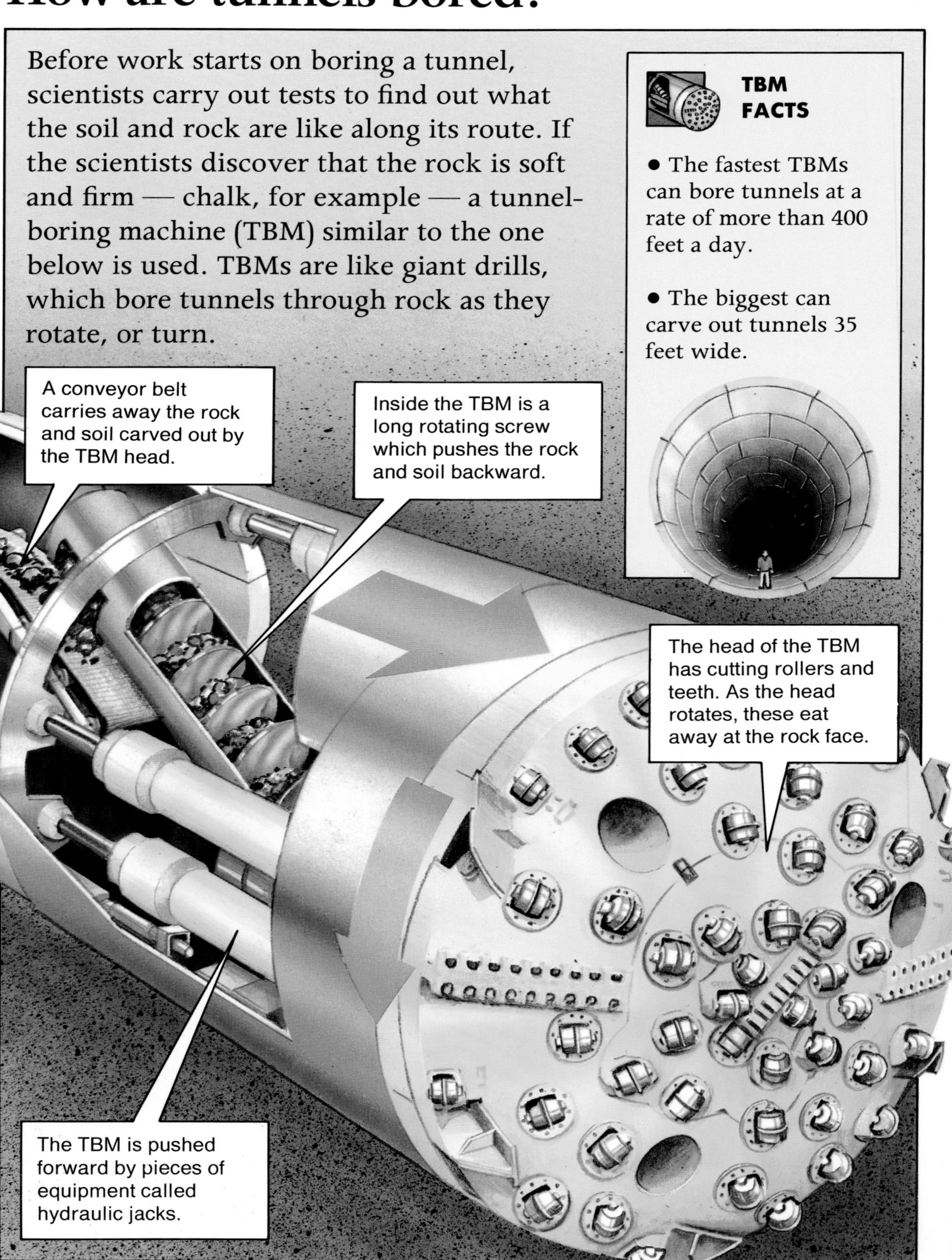

TBM FACTS

- The fastest TBMs can bore tunnels at a rate of more than 400 feet a day.
- The biggest can carve out tunnels 35 feet wide.

How are tunnels lined?

AIR SAFETY

When fresh air is pumped into tunnels for people to breathe, it helps to get rid of stale air and the exhaust fumes from cars at the same time. Try this experiment to see how fresh air can push out stale air.

1 Seal the ends of a cardboard tube with paper and sticky tape.

2 Make two holes in the tube, and push a bendy drinking straw into each one. Seal any gaps with modeling clay.

3 Angle one straw toward your cheek. Now put the other one in your mouth and blow — can you feel "stale" air being pushed out of the tube onto your cheek?

When a tunnel is bored through soft rock, it has to be lined to stop the roof and sides from collapsing. The linings are made from huge concrete or metal segments, which are lifted into position by machines as the TBM bores its way through the ground.

Gaps between the tunnel wall and lining segments are filled with concrete to seal the tunnel and make it watertight.

Lining segments are big and heavy, so machines are used to lift them into place.

When do tunnelers use explosives?

Some types of rock are much harder than others — coal is much harder than chalk, for example. If the route of a tunnel lies through very hard rock, workers blast their way through with explosives such as dynamite. Drills are mounted on a platform called a jumbo and used to make holes in the rock face. Explosives are placed in the holes and then detonated, or set off.

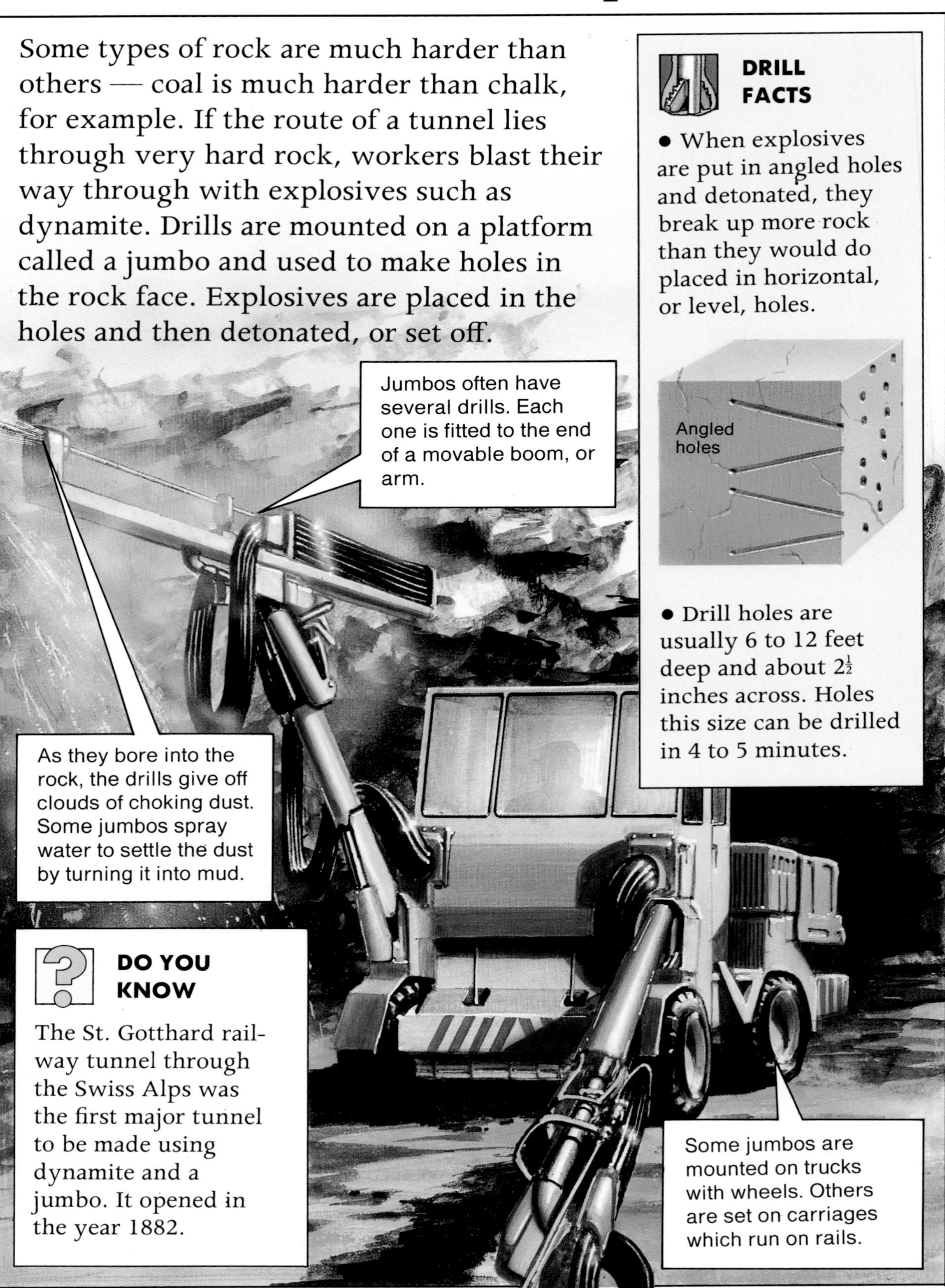

DRILL FACTS

- When explosives are put in angled holes and detonated, they break up more rock than they would do placed in horizontal, or level, holes.
- Drill holes are usually 6 to 12 feet deep and about $2\frac{1}{2}$ inches across. Holes this size can be drilled in 4 to 5 minutes.

DO YOU KNOW

The St. Gotthard railway tunnel through the Swiss Alps was the first major tunnel to be made using dynamite and a jumbo. It opened in the year 1882.

What are sunken-tube tunnels?

These are underwater tunnels which are built from huge metal or concrete tubes. The tubes are made in a factory, where they are sealed at both ends. Next they are taken to the tunnel site and towed into position by barges. Then they are lowered into a trench in the river or sea bed.

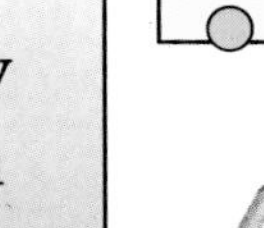

DO YOU KNOW

The BART (Bay Area Rapid Transit) underground railroad system includes the world's longest and deepest sunken-tube tunnels. Twin tunnels nearly 4 miles long are positioned about 130 feet below the surface of San Francisco Bay.

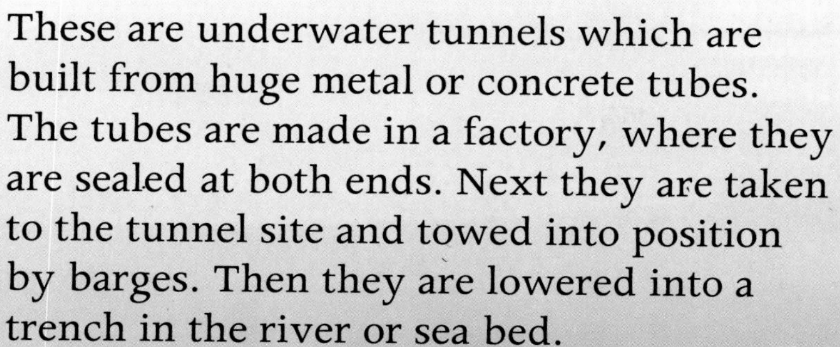

1 Barges are used to tow the tubes into position and lower them into a trench in the river or seabed.

2 Divers bolt the outside of the tubes together and seal the joins with concrete. They cover the tubes with sand and mud, to protect them.

3 Workers go inside the tubes to cut away the seals at each end. The tubes are then welded together to make one long water-tight tunnel.

DO YOU KNOW

Cut-and-cover is a method of building tunnels that don't have to be deep below the ground. Workers simply dig a trench, line it, and cover it up again.

Who built the first tunnels?

Tunneling began many thousands of years ago, when people dug holes to make the caves they lived in bigger. About 15,000 years ago, people started digging tunnels to mine a hard stone called flint for making tools and weapons.

DO YOU KNOW

The Romans built the first-known road tunnel over 2,000 years ago, in 36 B.C. It was near the city of Naples in southern Italy, and it was nearly a mile long.

About 3,500 years ago, after they stopped building pyramids, the Egyptians began making tombs like this by tunneling into soft rock. The tombs were decorated with beautiful wall paintings.

Where was the first subway built?

The world's first subway, or underground railway, was built in London and opened in 1863. At that time trains were pulled by steam locomotives. The first electric subway opened in London 27 years later.

SUBWAY FACTS

- The U.S.A.'s first subway opened in Boston in 1897.
- France's first subway, the Paris Métro, opened in 1900.
- The Moscow Metro, in the U.S.S.R., opened in the 1930s. Today it has the longest stretch of subway (nearly 20 miles long).

Which are the longest tunnels?

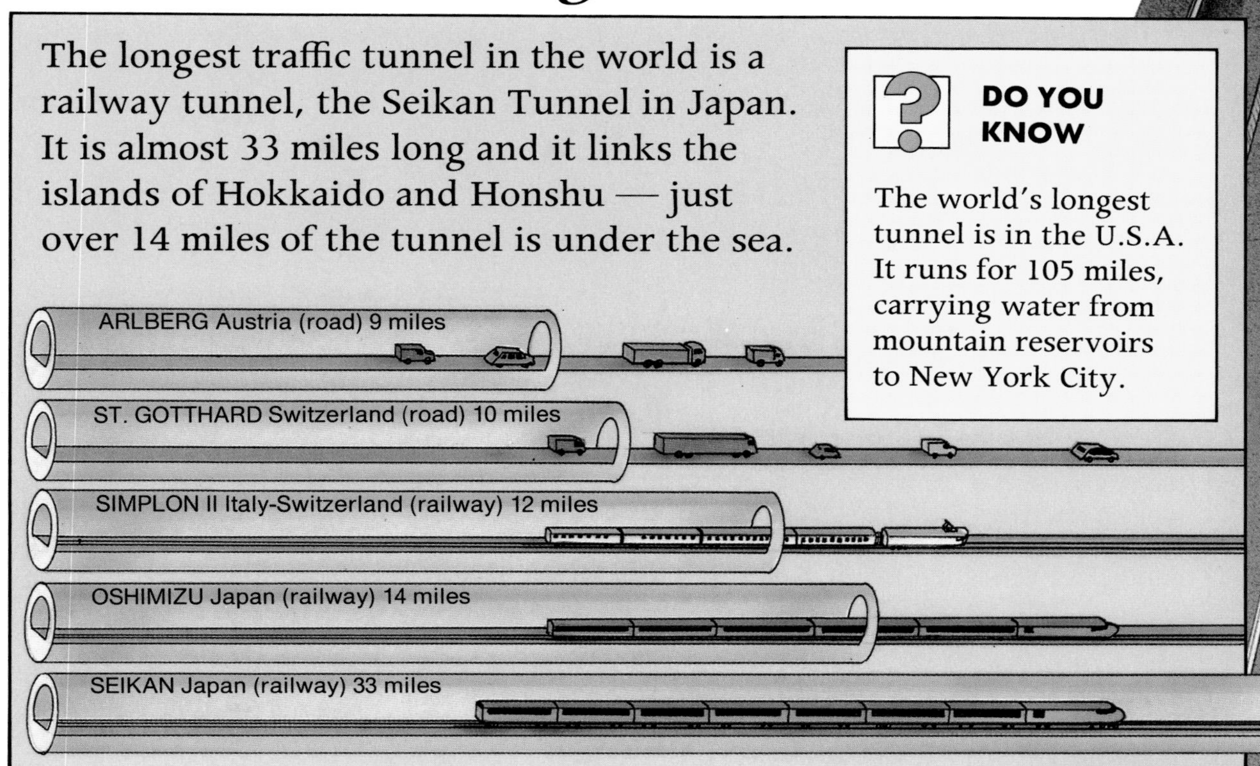

The longest traffic tunnel in the world is a railway tunnel, the Seikan Tunnel in Japan. It is almost 33 miles long and it links the islands of Hokkaido and Honshu — just over 14 miles of the tunnel is under the sea.

DO YOU KNOW

The world's longest tunnel is in the U.S.A. It runs for 105 miles, carrying water from mountain reservoirs to New York City.

Where are the deepest tunnels?

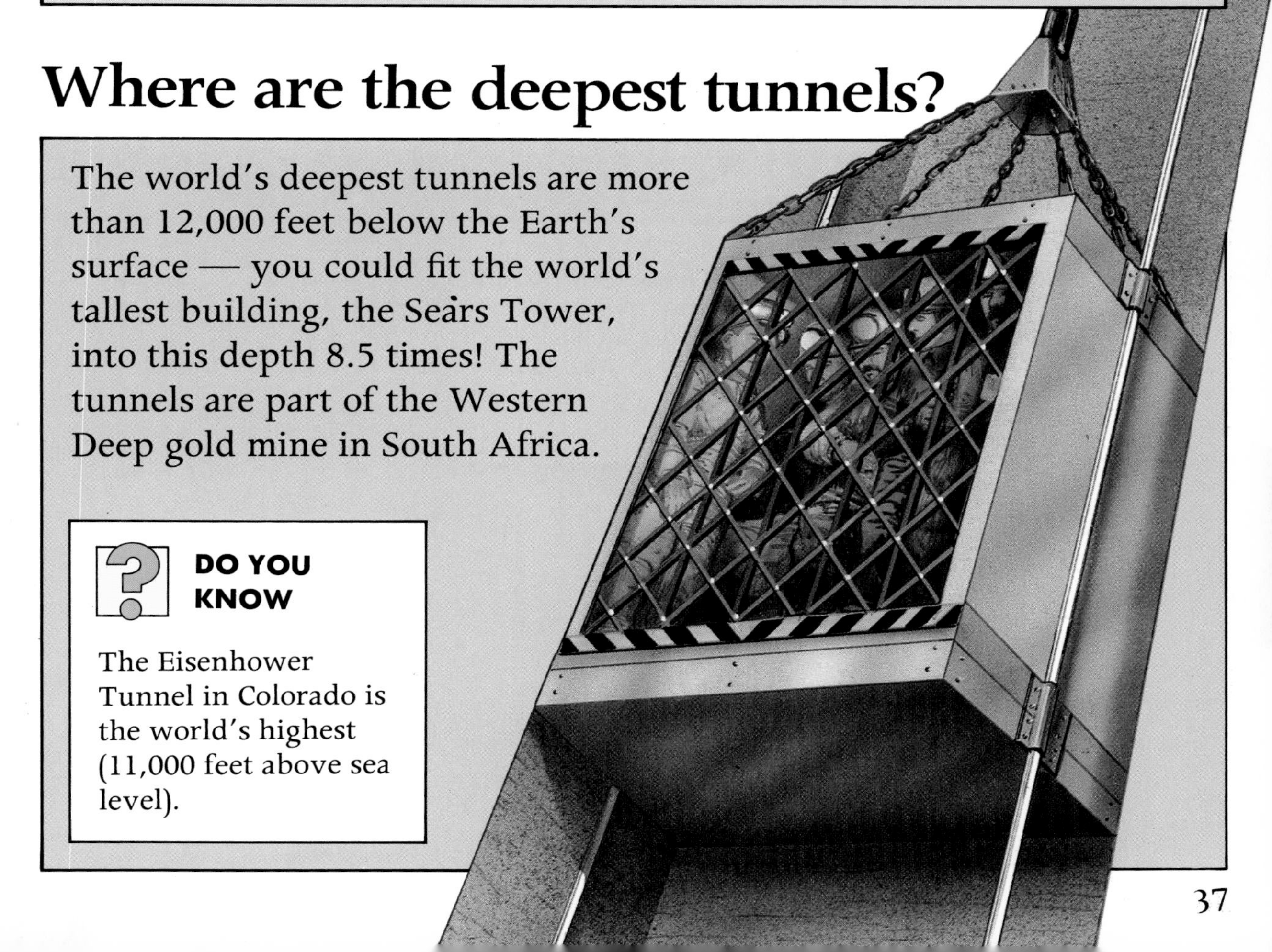

The world's deepest tunnels are more than 12,000 feet below the Earth's surface — you could fit the world's tallest building, the Sears Tower, into this depth 8.5 times! The tunnels are part of the Western Deep gold mine in South Africa.

DO YOU KNOW

The Eisenhower Tunnel in Colorado is the world's highest (11,000 feet above sea level).

What is the Eurotunnel?

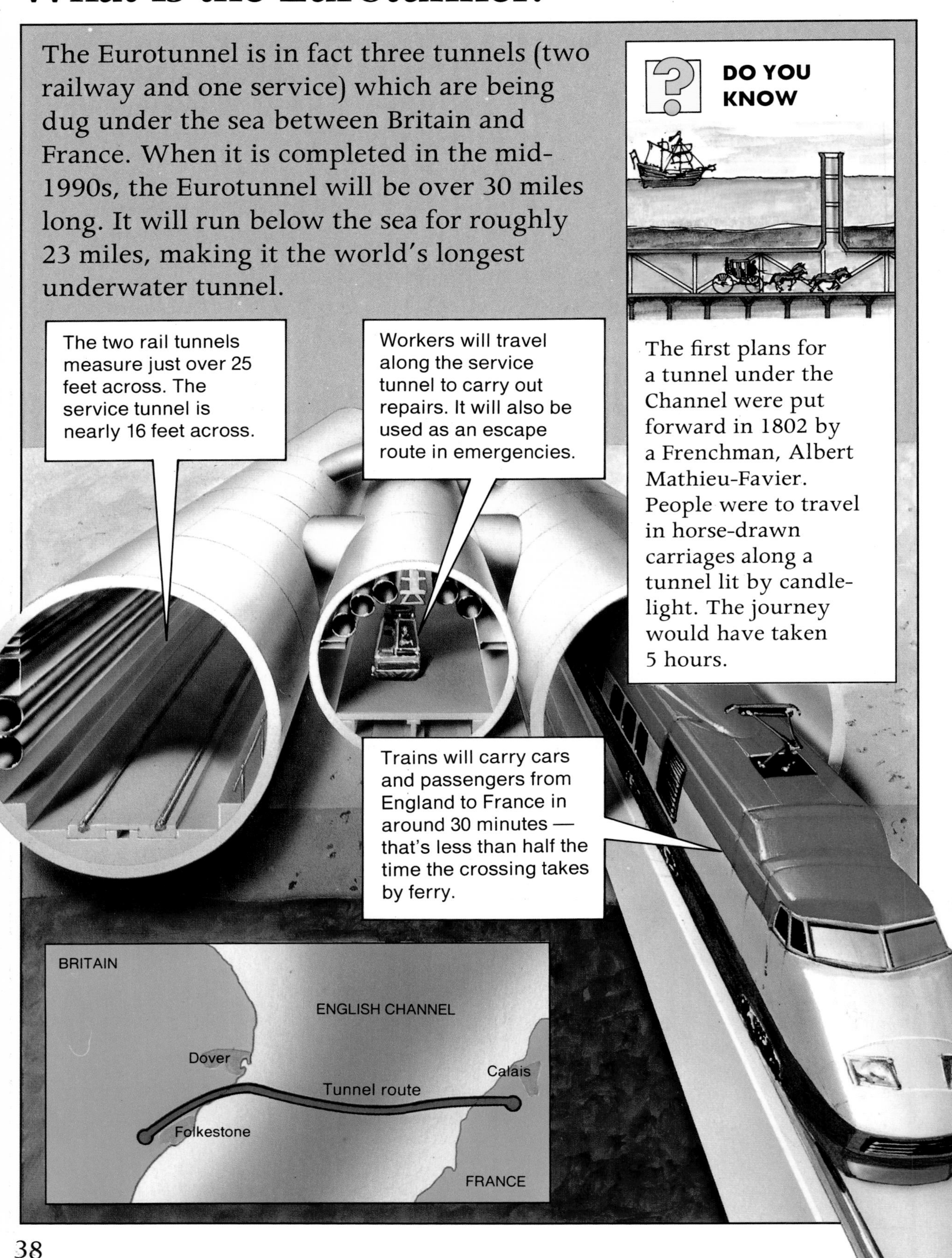

The Eurotunnel is in fact three tunnels (two railway and one service) which are being dug under the sea between Britain and France. When it is completed in the mid-1990s, the Eurotunnel will be over 30 miles long. It will run below the sea for roughly 23 miles, making it the world's longest underwater tunnel.

DO YOU KNOW

The first plans for a tunnel under the Channel were put forward in 1802 by a Frenchman, Albert Mathieu-Favier. People were to travel in horse-drawn carriages along a tunnel lit by candle-light. The journey would have taken 5 hours.

Useful words

Abutments The supports at each end of a bridge.

Architect Someone who designs buildings and draws up plans for them.

Cable A thick strong rope, often made from several metal wires twisted together.

Cement A building material made by mixing and burning clay and chalk, then grinding them into a fine powder. The powder becomes a paste when mixed with water, and the paste sets hard when it dries.

Concrete A very hard building material made by mixing sand, small stones or crushed rock, cement, and water — it sets like rock when it dries.

Deck The surface of a bridge — the part that carries the path, road, or railway.

Foundations The strong solid base on which a building or other structure rests. Foundations support the framework and stop heavy structures from sinking into soft ground.

Girder A long straight metal beam. Girders are usually made from steel.

Mortar A building material use in wall-building to stick bricks and stones together. It's made by mixing sand, cement, and water into a paste which dries hard. Lime is sometimes added to the paste.

Pier A vertical, or upright, support for the span of a bridge.

Reinforced concrete Concrete strengthened with metal rods.

Span The part of a bridge that lies between two supports (abutments, towers, or piers). The widest span is called the main span.

Story One level of a building.

Weld To join two pieces of metal by heating the edges until they melt and mix. A solid join forms when they cool.

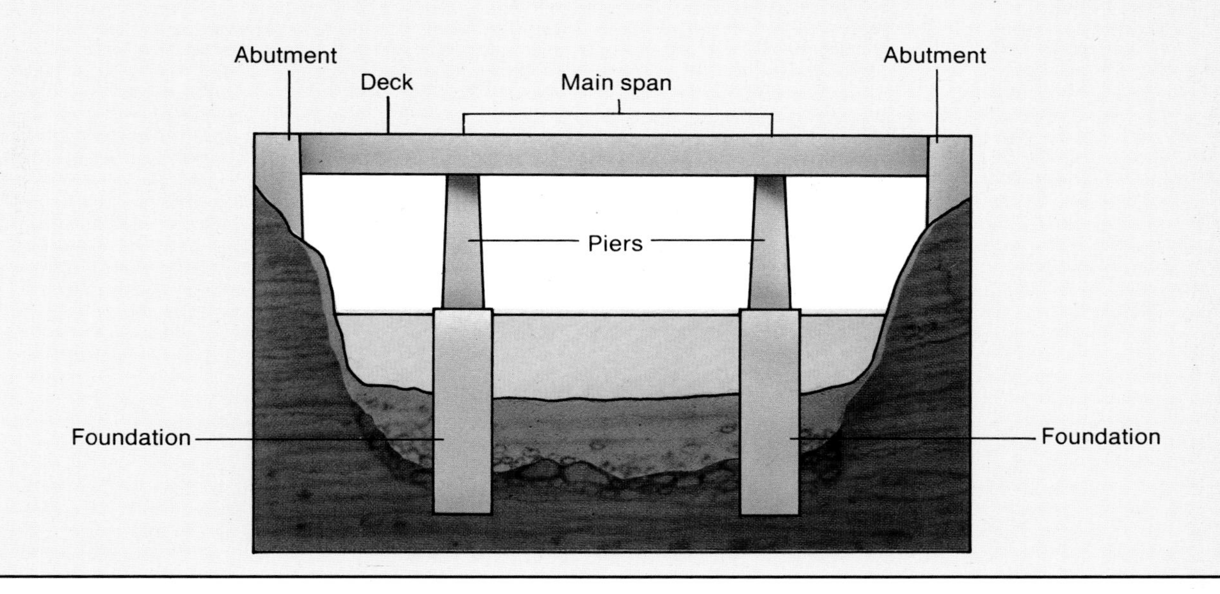

Index